BITTERSWEET

WHISPERS OF EXISTENCE

SATAKSHI PAGORE

Made with ❤ on the Notion Press Platform
www.notionpress.com

To my parents and family,

For being my greatest support and guiding me with love and wisdom.

To my cousins and my brother,

Who introduced me to the beauty of words and unknowingly shaped my love for literature.
For making sure I embraced English in every way, turning a habit into a passion.

To my friends,

For always motivating me with their strong words and kindness.

And to every reader who finds a piece of themselves in these pages—this book is for you.

Contents

Contents

Contents

Preface

Poetry has always been my way of understanding the world—a space where emotions flow freely, unburdened by the need for explanation. This book is not just a collection of poems but a reflection of my thoughts, experiences, and the small yet, profound moments that shape life.

This book focuses on the whispers of life and how everything is not perfect until you are satisfied, because happiness is the key for success.

I hope that as you read these poems, you find a piece of yourself in them. May they remind you of your own journey, your own emotions, and the beauty hidden in everyday life.

- Satakshi Pagore

Acknowledgements

Satakshi Pagore's love for English and literature blossomed when her cousin sister, Niharika, encouraged her to read an article every day. how her other cousin sister, Muktakshi, always made her watch movies in English, regardless of the Hindi dubbing. I am deeply grateful to my brother, Araadhvik, for teaching me the right words to uncover the world of literature, with every lesson on pronunciation and phrase, He has shaped my voice in countless ways. I credit my parents for nurturing her love for writing, as they have been my unwavering pillars of support, always ensuring I had everything I needed to follow her dreams. A heartfelt thank you to Lavanya didi for her help in designing the cover page and for consistently enriching my vocabulary with eloquent words, making me more articulate and knowledgeable.

What started as a simple habit soon became a deep passion, shaping her perspective and fueling her creativity to write this book and express her views out in the world.

Prologue

I have discovered that emotions don't always need to be voiced to be understood—sometimes, they are best expressed through the written word. So, whenever i felt wistful and melancholic, I grabbed my diary and a black pen, and started to whisper to the paper.

My poetry weaves together real and imagined experiences, drawing inspiration from the intricate layers of life. Though I come from a conservative family, I have always embraced the joy in simple, lighthearted moments, finding laughter in the smallest and stupidest things.

With this book, I aim to pour my emotions onto paper, offering my perspective on a wide range of topics and inviting the world to see 'life' through my eyes.

1. No Regrets

Tell them you love them, don't wait for the day,
for time is a thief, it won't let you stay.
A whisper unsaid, a hug never shared,
may turn into echoes of moments unspared.

You never quite know when a door softly closes,
when laughter fades, like the scent of old roses.
A place once familiar, a face once so near,
could vanish in time, like mist in the air.

So speak from your heart, let silence not win,
let love be the brush that paints from within.
Your life is your canvas—bold strokes, not confined,
no fear of tomorrow, no dreams left behind.

For what if the sun never rises the same?
What if the stars do not shine the same?
Live without chains, let your spirit be free,
No regrets, just a life as it's meant to be.

2. Warm Blanket

The words are lying on the floor,
waiting for someone to pick them up.
I do want to, possibly pick them up,
knit them into a blanket.
But,
I fear, it won't bring warmth,
only sorrow.

Yet still, they call to me,
begging to be held,
to be stitched into something whole.

I gather them, one by one,
threading them through trembling hands,
hoping they might cradle hearts,
not wound them.

But words are fragile,
and so are those who bear them.
Will they comfort, or will they cut?
Will they heal, or will they haunt?

I lay them down once more,

unsure if they belong in the open,
or if some things are meant
to remain unspoken.

3. A Sweet Lullaby

The moon hums a lullaby,
yet my limbs are heavy with longing,
not for sleep,
but for voices once bright.
Now,
tangled in silence,
lost in the night.

The night falls over me,
quiet like a stranger, watching, waiting.
The cold breeze carries whispers,
half-formed, unfinished,
like sentences left behind in a dream,
yet to be held by their lips.

I close my eyes,
not for sleep, not to rest,
hoping the night will return what it took,
even if only for a moment.

But the night is a keeper of secrets,
cloaked in silver and shadow,
offering only echoes,

never the touch of what once was.
The stars flicker like forgotten names,
calling softly,
but never quite reaching my hands.

I trace their glow with tired fingers,
each pulse a memory slipping away,
a thread unraveling in the hush of the dark.
The past lingers like mist on my skin,
soft, fading, just out of reach—
a lullaby I know but can no longer sing.

4. Always With Me, In My Heart.

I feel you near with me,
though in the stars.
Even on the days when loneliness
consumes me whole,
your presence is what I feel, soft and true.

Like warmth wrapped in summer air,
or silent steps upon the floor,
I turn to find you always there,
though you're not here,
yet evermore.

Through shadows deep and skies so wide,
in every breath, in every sigh,

I hear your voice in whispered leaves,
in echoes sung by midnight's breeze.
Your laughter hums in memory's thread,
a song unbroken, never dead.

I walk through places we once knew,
your footprints there, though faint and few.

The world has changed, the years have flown,
but never have I been alone.

But if you're here, in my heart,
then why can't I see you?
Hug you?
Talk to you?
Why does the silence answer in your place?
Why do my hands grasp only air,
when they reach for what's no longer there?

I really wish I hugged you a bit longer
the last time I saw you.
If I had known it was the last,
I would have held on,
memorized the rhythm of your heartbeat,
traced the warmth in your embrace,
let time stretch a little longer,
just to keep you close.

My biggest regret will always be
not spending enough time with you.
The missed moments, the unsaid words,
the laughter I thought we had time for,
all now folded into memory,
all now whispers in the wind.

You are the hush before the dawn,
the golden glow when night is gone.
You are the light, the quiet peace,
the tether time cannot release.

So even when the distance grows,
and life moves on in winding flows,
I close my eyes and feel you near,
not lost, not gone—just always here in my heart.

5. Silence Of The Dark

I hear a familiar tune woven into silence,
The silence holds what their words never could,
A quiet comfort, a fleeting peace.
I ask my reflection questions,
But it only stares back, offering nothing but silence in return.

What if my whole life was like this?
Endless questions, answers lost in the void,
A melody unfinished, a story untold.
It's 3 a.m., and my mind is heavy, clouded with what-ifs.
Still, I wait for the silence to break,
For answers to find me, or for me to find them.

The hours crawl, like whispers of forgotten dreams,
My thoughts swirl like autumn leaves in a breeze,
Tugged in directions I can't control.

Where do the words go, when they fade into the night?
Where do the hopes vanish, when they slip through my fingers?
I hear my heart beat, but even that feels distant,
A rhythm that keeps time but never moves me forward.
And still, I wait.

The walls are thick with unspoken truths,
The air dense with everything we never said,
The questions building up, stacking high,
A tower of what-ifs, reaching for the stars,
But never quite touching them.

I long for a sign, a flicker of light in the dark,
To shatter this quiet and show me the way.
But all I have is the silence,
And the weight of words that never came.
And so, I sit,
The world outside asleep,
While I wait for the silence to break,
Hoping the answers will find me before the dawn.

6. Forgotten Smiles

You can always tell if someone is not okay,
but people around me just ignore that fact.
They like to make jokes on it,
they like to laugh it off.

You can always tell if someone's not okay,
in the way their laughter falters, fades away.
Eyes that sparkle hold shadows unseen,
hiding stories behind where they've been.

Their smiles may come on their faces, but not meet their eyes,
a storm lies quiet beneath sunny skies.
The words they speak are crafted with care,
but between the lines, there's a crack, a tear.

They might say, "I'm fine," with a trembling tone,
yet carry the weight of battles unknown.
Shoulders droop from the burden they bear,
though they'll say they're strong, their silence will share.

It's in the way they pause before they reply,
the distant gaze, the quiet sigh.
How their hands fidget, their posture tight,

the way they linger in the quiet of night.

So look beyond the surface they show,
be gentle, be kind, for you may not know
The battles they fight, the pain they conceal,
sometimes the smallest cracks reveal what's real.

The world is cruel and cold.
So,
offer a word, a shoulder, a stay.
Sometimes, love is the light in their grey.

For you can always tell, if you dare to see,
that someone's not okay,
but longs to be free.

7. 2019

I hate the child I once was,
the nine-year-old who learned too soon,
to bottle up her storms,
to hide her pain behind quiet smiles.
To swallow her words,
she learnt to lock her feelings away,
in a rusted chest.

Anger, pain, anxiety, doubt,
she carried them all.
Stacked them like bricks around her heart,
building walls too high to climb.
Unable to allow anyone to enter,
she closed herself inside walls and a ceiling.

She smiled when she was meant to,
laughed when the world expected.
But inside, she shrank,
drowning in the weight of unspoken storms.

I wish I could reach back,
hold her hand,
hug her tight.

Tell her that, it was okay to cry,
to scream, to feel, to be.

But all I can do is whisper now,
to my 2019 self.
Softly, into the silence she left behind,
hoping she hears me,
hoping she forgives me.

8. How To Disappear?

How do you disappear?
Without hurting someone?
Without leaving empty spaces behind?
without your absence,
feeling like a hollowed-out home?

I wonder,
if I ever fade into silence,
Will someone strain to hear me?
if I ever step away slowly,
will someone reach for a hand,
that is no longer there?

I don't want to be an echo,
of something once loved.
A missing piece
that turns whole hearts heavy.

So I stay,
half here.
Caught between wanting to vanish,
and fearing the 'ache' I'd leave behind.

So,

I ask myself again,

How do you disappear? Without hurting anyone?

9. Puzzle Pieces

We are like two puzzle pieces,
Imperfect alone, yet fate releases
A bond so rare, a love so true,
No one else could fit like you.

Edges worn, yet made to mend,
Not just love, but best of friends.
Through every crack, through every scar,
You found me where the broken pieces are.

Apart, we're lost, not quite whole,
Incomplete in heart and soul.
But side by side, we lock in tight,
Two puzzle pieces, made just right.

Through storms that rage, through endless night,
Through whispered doubts, through fading light,
We hold on tight, we do not fall,
For even broken, we have it all.

The world may shift, the tides may turn,
The stars may fade, the heavens burn,
But still we stand, hand in hand,

Two hearts that time cannot unplan.

Some call it fate, some call it chance,
A fleeting step in life's own dance.
But we were carved to fit this way,
To find each other, come what may.

Through laughter bright and silent cries,
Through whispered truths and soft goodbyes,
We've walked through fire, we've braved the rain,
Yet always found our way again.

When distance tries to pull apart
The puzzle bound within our heart,
We'll find our way, we'll bridge the space,
For nothing else could take your place.

And when the years have come and gone,
When memories fade but love holds on,
We'll still remain, through space and time,
Two puzzle pieces—yours and mine.

Even if edges start to fray,
If colors dim and time turns gray,
Still, side by side, we will remain,
Two halves that form a whole again.

10. Drained

I have been telling them,
for days, for weeks,
that my eyes have lost their spark.
That the light once dancing within them,
has flickered, faded, disappeared.

The eyes that once glowed,
with the warmth of laughter,
with dreams spun from golden threads.
Now glisten with quiet sorrow,
reflecting only the dim glow of the night.

They do not shine with wonder,
nor shimmer with stories untold.
They carry the weight of unspoken words,
of silent battles, of echoes left unheard.

I search for the girl I used to be,
the one whose gaze held the sunrise.
But all I see is a stranger,
blinking back with tears,
in the dark.

11. 11:11

I wanted to give up on everything,
everything except you.
I could have walked away,
let the weight of it pull me under,
but you stayed.
And that was enough to keep me here.

I don't mean to hold you so tightly
that you can't breathe.
I just don't know how to be there for you,
without wanting you with me always,
without fearing the space between us
might turn into distance.

If I lose you, my world will break and shatter into a billion
pieces ,
but that doesn't mean I'd stop waiting.
I'd wait in every quiet moment,
in every whispered prayer,
where your name echoes long after it's spoken.

Because loving you isn't a choice,
it's the air I breathe,

because loving you is like breathing, and how can I ever stop
breathing?
the wish I make when the clock hits 11:11,
the forever I hope for,
even when forever feels uncertain.

Staying forever,
that's all I want.
Not just for now, not just for a while,
but for as long as time allows.

12. YOU

You have to be thing that saves you.
the world won't wait for you,
it doesn't stop spinning when,
you re-open your wounds,
and it doesn't stop spinning when,
you're curled up in a ball, on the floor.

NO ONE IS COMING TO RESCUE YOU

The world may not always be kind to you,
but you can be.
You can be kind to yourself.
You need to stand up to the sun that still rises,
and you can too.

On the days, when sadness swallows you whole,
and you have cemented yourself to the bed, you have to get
up.
There are many things in this world which are evil,
but you are not one of them.

The tears won't stop,
because,

the world is cold and unforgiving.

BE YOUR OWN HERO.
because,
the only thing that will ever save you,
is YOU.

13. Under The Weight Of Childhood Reminisce

Her childhood self,
dreamed in colors too bright to fade,
believed in kindness like an unbroken thread.
Hoped to be the happiest person alive,
not knowing the future had other plans.

She grew up learning that smiles could'nt lie,
that not every hand reaching out
was meant to hold her safely.
The world taught her to guard her heart,
So,
she laid down, brick by brick,
to build walls where once there were open doors.

She had to become selfish,
not out of greed,
but to keep herself from breaking,
to survive in a world that took too much,
and gave too little in return.

Yet somewhere deep inside,
her old self still lingers.

She wonders if she lost herself in survival,
or if she was simply forced to change.

There's a place I go in the still of the night,
Where the world was simple, and hearts were light.
A time when the grass was greener, the sky was wide,
And every dream felt like a wave I could ride.

I remember the laughter that rang through the air,
The warmth of the sun on days without care.
Barefoot and free, I'd run through the streets,
The sound of my footsteps a rhythm so sweet.

Old treehouses stood like castles in the sky,
Where secrets were whispered, where time passed by.
I'd hold the world in my small, eager hands,
Building kingdoms from dirt, making castles in the sand.

The taste of ice cream on a hot summer day,
The way time seemed endless, like it would never stray.
I'd chase the fireflies, catch them in jars,
Pretend I could touch the moon, reach the stars.

But childhood is fleeting, like a breath in the wind,
A fleeting moment that you can never fully pin.
Still, in my heart, it forever remains—
The joy of those days, the freedom that sustains.

Now I look back with a bittersweet smile,
Wishing for just one more innocent mile.
But the memories stay, tucked deep inside,
A treasure of moments that time can't divide.

14. I Miss You

I miss people dealing with me, with patience.
How you patiently, sat with me,
and taught me the spelling of 'milkshake',
gently guiding me through each alphabet.
you never got tired, never gave up.

I miss people dealing with me, with care.
How you always defended me in front of mumma,
and took the blame for something you didn't do,
knowing that I was wrong, you always shielded me.

I miss people dealing with me, with love.
How you used to give me your favourite chocolates,
just to see my face light up,
you sacrificed your joys.

I miss people dealing with me, with softness.
How you played with me,
even though I broke rules, even when I tested your limits.

I miss people dealing with me, with laughter.
How you exactly knew how to make me smile,
even after making me angry.

I miss every single thing about you.

15. Choice

I chose you yesterday,
when the world was quiet
and love felt easy.
When laughter was endless,
and time moved gently,
carrying us like a soft breeze
through sunlit days and starry nights.

I choose you today,
even when life is messy,
even when the days feel heavy.
Through the storms and the silence,
through the moments of doubt,
when words fail and hearts ache,
I still reach for you,
still hold you close.

And I will choose you tomorrow,
no matter what comes,
no matter where this road takes us.
Through distance, through change,
through the unknown that waits ahead—
my heart will not waver,

my love will not fade.

Because love isn't just a feeling,
it's a choice.
A promise in the dark,
a vow renewed with every sunrise,
a steady hand, a quiet strength,
a light that never dims.

And every single day,
I will choose you.
In joy and in sorrow,
in certainty and in fear,
through every season,
through every year.

Again and again.
Always.

16. Shades Of Life

Don't paint me pictures of dreams so bright,
if they'll fade like stars in the morning light.
Why whisper of dawn with a silver hue,
if the sky you left me is empty and blue?

Why couldn't you pick a different shade,
a touch of lavender, or a hint of jade?
Why must my soul, once open and free,
be drowning in waves you left inside me?

You held the brush, you had the choice,
yet colored my world in a voiceless voice.
No crimson of love, no gold embrace,
just endless blue in a hollowed space.

So take back the dreams, the hues that bleed,
erase the echoes that fill my head.
If all you could give was a sky turned cold,
I'd rather be colorless than be painted in gold.

But still, the past stains like ink on my skin,
each memory carved, each whisper within.
The colors you left may never fade,

but I refuse to live in the shade you made.

So I'll take the brush with trembling hands,
rewrite the story, redraw the strands.
I'll no longer be trapped in the hues you chose,
I'll paint my world in colors that glow.

Let the crimson love and my golden light,
break through the storm, dissolve the night.
And if the past still lingers near,
I'll turn my pain into something clear.

For even the darkest shades can blend,
can shift, can change, can somehow mend.
And though you made me feel lost, undone, but,
my masterpiece has just begun.

17. Echoes Of The Unseen

The night is silent, yet it screams,
a restless tide of shattered dreams.
a weightless ache, yet heavy.
Still,
a war within, a mind unfilled.

The world moves on, the sun still burns,
yet my light is lost in twists and turns.
smiles feel borrowed, laughter strained,
hope a whisper, love restrained,

In the quiet, where shadows play,
There are echoes of the unseen, drifting away.
Whispers that linger, just out of reach,
A silent language no one can teach.

They dance in the corners of empty rooms,
Fading like sunlight in morning's gloom.
You can't hear them, but you can feel—
A soft hum, a tremor, an echo that's real.

They are the moments that slip through time,

The unspoken words, the unsung rhyme.
The space between breaths, the things left behind,
The traces of thought that slip from the mind.

The unseen carries stories untold,
Of dreams that shatter, of hearts that unfold,
Of love that never quite touched the air,
Of burdens too heavy, too hard to bear.

In every pause, in every sigh,
The echoes of the unseen never die.
They linger in silence, in shadows, in sound,
In the quietest corners, where truths are found.

"Be strong" they say,
yet strength dissolves in endless nights.
I wear a mask, I play my part.

But, even storms must bow to time,
and the darkest of nights will yield to shine.
so i hold on, though torn apart,
waiting for dawn, to mend my heart.

18. In The Stars

I search for you in the bereft night,
where moonlight spills its silver light.
The world is still, yet I can feel
a presence soft, yet bright and real.

The stars above don't seem so far,
for maybe now, you are a star.
Maybe you're the brightest one,
the steady glow when day is done.
I close my eyes and see your face,
a love that time cannot erase.

Though life was cruel and took you soon,
it left me pieces, left me clues—
a laugh that lingers in my mind,
a warmth that distance cannot lose.
A bond unbroken, tried, and true,
it's still just me, and still just you.

I speak your name, and though it aches,
it brings you closer, never fades.
Not gone, not lost, not far away,
you live in me, you'll always stay.

I see you in the golden dawn,
in every bird that sings its song.
In rustling leaves, in ocean waves,
in all the love you freely gave.

So when the night feels dark and long,
I'll hear you in the wind's soft song.
When I look up, near or far,
I'll find you shining in a star.

And though my hands can't hold you tight,
you're with me still, in love and light.
Not just a memory, not just a dream—
but part of all I've ever been.

19. Light Within

When shadows whisper, cold and deep,
and silence lulls your soul to sleep,
when hope feels like a distant star,
too faint to see, too far to grasp.

Breathe, my love, and don't let go,
there's warmth beyond what sorrow shows.
Even when the night feels long,
the world still hums its quiet song.

Seek the light, though dim it glows,
in laughter shared, in hands that hold,
in stories told, in love that stays,
in golden dawns and softer days.

The world still holds a place for you,
with skies so vast,
And even if the clouds draw near,
they'll pass—the sky will still be clear.

Hold on tight, don't be afraid,
your soul is strong, your light won't fade.
For even in the darkest night,

within you burns a boundless light.

You are not broken, not undone,
you are not lost—you are the sun.

Even when the road is steep,
even when your heart must weep,

Know this: you are not alone.
Your heart still beats, your strength has grown.
The storm may rage, the night may call,
but you were born to rise, not fall.

So take my hand, and take a breath,
there's still so much of life left yet.
You shine, my love, you always will,
the light within you, bright still.

20. The Need To Scream

Have you ever felt a voice inside,
clawing, burning, aching wide?
A sound too loud to stay unseen,
yet trapped beneath where no one sees.

The world moves fast, and skips my name,
I'm here, yet absent, just the same.
A fleeting shadow, unheard call,
a whisper drowned beneath it all.

I speak, but the silence swallows me whole,
my words dissolve, they have no hold.
I reach for hands that never stay,
I stand in crowds, but drift away.

So I hold it back, the words, the fire,
a caged storm, a buried pyre.
I smile, I nod, I play the part,
while thunder echoes in my heart.

But even embers softly gleam—
maybe it's time to finally scream.
Not for sorrow, not for fear,

but just to say: I'm truly here.

Let the world hear what I've kept inside,
the silent wars, the dreams denied.
Let my voice rise, fierce and bright,
like lightning tearing through the night.

Because I am real, I am seen,
not just a thought, not just between.
No longer waiting, no longer small—
I am here, and that is all.

21. First Glance

I remember the first time we met,
glances shared across the room,
unspoken words lingering in the air.
I remember thinking you were awfully mean,
and you probably thought I was awfully quiet.

Yet, something unseen pulled us near,
a thread woven by time, delicate yet strong.
Maybe the universe wanted us to know
that we were meant to be forever,
that this was destiny calling our names.

Honestly, I wonder where I would be without you—
without your laughter echoing in my quietest days,
without your presence, a warmth I never knew I needed.
We are like roots intertwined beneath the ground,
silent strength in the ties we have found.

You are the lighthouse to my stormy sea,
the steady glow guiding me home.
The constant stars aligned,
a love written in constellations long before we met.

Through seasons that change, through time that flies,
through distance and silence, through tears and goodbyes,
here we stand, our bond forever true.
From that first glance,
to every moment after—
it has always been me and you.

22. To Be Known, Is To Be Loved

To be loved is to be known,
but why do I still feel unseen?
Like a voice lost,
like a name no one remembers.

I walk through crowds, I laugh, I speak,
yet something in me stays unheard.
A quiet ache, a whispered wish—
to be understood, to truly belong.

I don't want love that comes and goes,
that flickers out when the days get cold.
I want someone to stay, to see,
to hear the things I never say aloud.

To notice when my smile is forced,
to know the weight I sometimes hold.
Not passing glances, not half-meant words,
but something real, something whole.

Stand by me when the rain pours down,
when the world turns silent, heavy, grey.

Be the warmth when winter stays too long,
the steady light when I lose my way.

If you hear this quiet plea,
stay. Listen. Let me be seen.
Not as an afterthought, not as a ghost,
but as someone who matters the most.

Call my name and mean it.
Take my hand and don't let go.
Because to be loved is to be known,
and all I've ever wanted
was to be known as me.

23. The Essence Of Love

Love exists in every form,

A gentle touch,

a heart so warm.

It binds the souls, both far and near,

A whispered word,

a fallen tear.

No name, love needs

no rule it keeps,

It finds us all,

it runs so deep.

Though some may call it overhyped,

Love is real,

both wrong and right.

It happens to all of us,

no matter what age,

or what place.

Complete or not,

it leaves a mark,

A guiding light within the dark.

For without love,

we'd fade away,
Like night that never meets the day.

24. Home?

Where do I go when home feels strange,
When walls once safe now shift and change?
The echoes call, but not my name,
A place I love, yet not the same.

Do I stay and play my part,
A quiet ghost with a heavy heart?
Do I smile, pretend, endure the show,
While something in me longs to go?

Or do I run, chase open skies,
Let the wind unmask the lies?
Find a place where hearts beat free,
Where home is more than memory.

But maybe home is not a space,
Not just walls, not just a place.
Maybe home's a heart that stays,
Through every loss, through every fray.

A star that can't call the sky it's home, A leaf that feels
abandoned by its own tree.
A bird that soars but fears the sky.

Why do I feel so lost?
When I seem like I have a map in my hand?
The path I walk, seems worn.
each step, leaves me torn.
The very thing that should bring me peace,
gives me nothing but grief.

Four walls, that close in tight,
turn days into endless nights.
The silence in my mind is so loud.
A constant heavy shroud.

Why do I feel like I'm only a daughter, a girl who shares the
blood she didn't ask for.
I stand in a house, which I'm afraid isn't my own.
A place where, I've never truly grown. trapped in a role,
which I didn't choose but,
in a place which I can't lose.

So where I go, I do not know,
But I'll find warmth where love can grow.

25. A Dying Hope

Before,
I had something inside me—
a fire, a spark, a reason to move.
It kept me warm, kept me believing,
made me feel like I could be something.

Now,
it's just… gone.
The spark that once lit me up
is nowhere to be found.
And I sit here, on the edge of my bed,
staring at nothing,
wishing things were different.

26. Unwritten For Now,

The most beautiful things about you,
are the ones you'll never see,
the way your laughter lingers soft,
like echoes on the sea.

The way your lips, so unaware,
speak kindness without a sound,
how your presence feels like poetry,
where lost souls are found.

Each day I read you, page by page,
a story yet untold,
a book untouched by any hands,
yet worth more than gold.

Every glance and every smile,
Is a line that never fades,
A story that stretches mile by mile.

Your quiet strength, unseen, untold,
Whispers through the silent air,
A tale of courage, brave and bold,
That no one else could ever wear.

The way your soul can light the dark,
A flicker that turns into flame,
Unseen, but felt like a quiet spark,
A light that never seeks acclaim.

I turn each page with bated breath,
Not knowing where it ends or starts,
Each chapter feels like life and death,
A journey written in our hearts.

So here's my pen, an open page,
For all the words you cannot see,
Together we'll write through every age,
In this unwritten book, just you and me.

And though you'll never truly know,
the beauty that I see,
I'll cherish every word of you,
a love only meant for me and you.

27. Reflections In The Mirror

I stand before the mirror's gaze,
tracing stories on my face.
Each scar, each tear, a tale untold,
of battles fought, of hands left cold.

I am proof that storms will fade,
that the sun still rises, though skies have swayed.
No matter how the tempests rise,
I choose to walk, not close my eyes.

For running never sets you free,
it chains the soul in misery.
But standing firm, though fears remain,
is how the heart unlearns its pain.

So I will walk through fire and rain,
through love, through loss, through joy and pain.
For life will turn, the tides will shift,
and every wound will heal, a gift.

I stand before the glass,
A stranger's face in a silent stare,

The reflection is mine, yet it feels distant,
Like a memory I can't quite repair.

Eyes that hold stories I've never told,
Lips that whisper secrets I don't know,
A face shaped by time, by choices, by chance,
But still, I wonder—who's this in the glance?

The mirror shows more than just skin deep,
It holds the parts I hide and keep,
A reflection of thoughts, of dreams and fears,
Of laughter, of heartache, of unshed tears.

I ask the glass, "Who are you to me?"
But it only reflects what it chooses to see.
The cracks in the smile, the shadows in sight,
The silent questions that linger at night.

It's both a friend and a foe in disguise,
A place where I seek, where I search, where I try,
To find the truth in a world made of glass,
To understand the future, to let go of the past.

One day, the fairytale will start,
not in escape, but in my life.

28. To My Mumma, My Wonderwoman

Mumma,

I still cherish the way you've always been my safe place,
the one who listens, who understands,
who makes everything feel right with just a look.
Even in the quiet, I know your love surrounds me.

Your presence is my comfort, your care my strength.
I see it in the smallest things—
the way you remember what I love,
the way you're always there, even without words.

We've both grown, in ways big and small,
but one thing will never change—
you will always be my heart's happiest place,
my forever home.

But Mumma, I hope you always know,
that,
you are my endless cheer,
My love for you grows every year.
No words enough, no way to show,

Your laughter rings like sweetest songs,
a melody where I belong.
Your hands have held my smallest fears,
wiped away my endless tears

No words could hold the love I feel,
no poem could make it all seem real.
But know this, Mumma, pure and true,
the happiest part of me is you.

I love you so much, more than I can ever tell.

29. To My Papa, My Superhero

Papa,

I don't know when time flew by,
when I grew up, and so did you.
But through every change, every day,
your love has always shone through.

You're here, you're near, you always stay,
with stories to tell, come what may.
Your words, your laughter, your gentle cheer,
make every worry disappear.

With you, no dream feels out of sight,
no road too tough, no climb too high.
You've always been my strongest guide,
my shelter, my hope, my endless pride.

From tiny toys to midnight treats,
to silly things I didn't need,
yet still, you smiled and said, "Why not?"
and gave me all the love you've got.

You work so hard, yet never show
the weight you carry, the miles you go.
For every wish, for every plan,
you always say, "Don't worry—I can."

No treasure shines, no star above,
can match my Papa's endless love.
For all you do, for all you are,
you'll always be my guiding star.

Papa, you are my joy, my pride,
my strength, my laughter, my safest side.
Forever grateful, forever free,
because of all you give to me.

So stay here, tell me stories of when you were a kid,
let's laugh and talk just like we did.
Let's fill the air with warmth and fun,
because with you, life's always bright as the sun.

And I love you—more than words can say,
today, tomorrow, and every day.

30. More Than Just Cousins

They say cousins are just family by name,
But to me, they're home, they're love, they're the same.
Not just by blood, but by heart, by choice,
The ones who understand me without a voice.

Muktakshi didi, my safe little space,
She spoils me rotten with love and grace.
We share the same cravings, the same little dreams,
She's as pretty as a Pinterest board, and even more.

Niharika didi, my partner in crime,
Movie nights that turn into nap time.
Her style, her laughter, the way she just gets me,
With her, every moment is light and free.

Tavish bhaiya, my guide, my friend,
With Maggi and chocolate walks that never end.
He lets me win, but teaches me too,
A brother so rare, so kind, so true.

Apoorva didi, my laughter untamed,
Where stupid jokes never feel lame.

At nani's house, with gossip to share,
She listens, she laughs—she's always there.

And then there's Dolsee, my little one,
Who I teach, who I scold, but it's all in fun.
A sister to guide, to love, to adore,
With her, life is never a bore.

Suhani didi, road trip queen,
Laughing at jokes that shouldn't be seen.
Food and games, your endless cheer,
With you, my world feels clear.

And then there's Lavanya didi, my twin,
Late-night talks and gossip begin.
She yaps, she listens, she knows me best,
A role model I admire.

Even though I have so many cousins,I am grateful for each
and everyone of them, but these people are even more
precious than gold.

So here's to them, my heart, my home,
The ones who make sure I'm never alone.
Not just cousins, but more,
so much more.

The family I cherish, the love I adore.

31. To My Second Parents, My Grandparents

There's a kind of love, so warm, so true,
A love that stays, no matter what I do.
It lives in their smiles, their gentle embrace,
In every small moment, in every safe place.

Nani, with hugs so soft, so tight,
Kisses my cheeks, makes my world bright.
She knows my favorites, my little delights,
From Diwali's crackers to Holi's fights.

Nanu, my guide, my biggest fan,
Teaches me wisdom,
We crave the same food, our hearts align,
And Nani makes sure her food is always divine.

Amma, the one who spoils me best,
Gives me all, from toys to the rest.
Even a diamond, if I wished so,
Just to see my face glow.

She taught me colors, to paint and create,
To keep things neat, to never be late.

Yet through it all, her love stays pure,
A bond so strong, steady, and sure.

They are my home, my heart, my light,
The ones who make my world feel right.
And if love is measured in all that they do,
Then I hope they know,
I love them too.

32. Forever People AKA Family

Here is to the parts of my family, other than my wonderful parents,

To my bua(Nupur), so strong and true,
With courage bright, you always push through.
You inspire me to heal and care,
To chase my dreams, to always dare.
Through every storm, you stand so tall,
Your love, the greatest gift of all.

To tauji(Karunesh) and taiji(Ritika), warm and kind,
A love so pure, so rare to find.
Dinners, trips, and sweet delights,
Turning days to joyful nights.
Taiji's food, a hug so sweet,
Tauji's words, a love complete.

To my mausi(Deepti), my partner in crime,
With every chat, we lose track of time.
The best at hearing all I say,
Laughing with me along the way.
And my mausa(Navneet), a chef so grand,

Spreading joy with a loving hand.

To mami(Ruchi)and mama(Vaibhav)
my special two,
With silent games and laughs so true.
Mami, you take me near and far,
For things that live within my heart.
Mama, our 'sandwich' and 'kesari' jokes will never fade,
A bond so strong, forever made.

Each of you, a part of me,
A bond unbreakable as can be.
Through love and care, through thick and thin,
With you all, my heart will always win.

33. Drowning In Your Shadows

I'd rather drown in your shadows,
than swim in someone else's light.
For even in the darkest corners,
you are my warmth, my quiet night.

Let the world shine all around me,
let it call me to its glow,
but I'd rather stand beside you,
in the only love I know.

Your silence speaks in echoes,
your presence hums so low,
yet even in the stillness,
it's the only home I know.

The world may offer brighter paths,
soft hands, a gentler way,
but they don't know the way you hold me,
or the words you never say.

The night may stretch before us,
long and endless, deep and wide,

but I will never fear the darkness,
with your heartbeat by my side.

So let me fade into your darkness,
let me sink into your hue,
for I'd rather drown in your shadows,
than shine in light not meant for me.

34. Aadya, My Ride Or Die

Since we were five,
Side by side, we've learned to stand.
Through every laugh, through every tear,
You've been my constant, always near.

You listen, even when words are few,
No need for answers, just being you.
From endless gossip to silly fights,
Every moment with you feels right.

You're not just my bestfriend; you're my heart,
A bond so strong, never apart.
Everyone knows, they see it too,
My world feels whole because of you.

We aren't 5 year old kids anymore,
But we still laugh on the same joke we made to eachother
when we were 5.
I realise, that a part of us,
will always be those little girls.

It's something that will never leave us,

like a shadow which will always follow us.

Aadya, you'll always be family to me.

You're my nemo,
if you ever get lost in the great big ocean,
I'll always find you.

35. Rishita, My Soul Sister

Through sun and rain,
We've weathered all, through joy and pain.
Though life once tried to pull us far,
You've always been my guiding star.

At twelve, we found our way again,
Like missing pieces, my dearest friend.

You know my thoughts before I speak,
My silent words, the truths I keep.

A single glance, and you just know,
A bond so rare, so strong, so true,
Rishita, I'd be lost without you.

In every chapter, every page,
We've danced through every storm and stage.
Through laughter loud and quiet sighs,
We've seen the world through each other's eyes.

Through sleepless nights and endless talks,
Through paths we walked and afternoon walks,

No matter what the world may throw,
We've always found a way to grow.

From childhood dreams to adult fears,
Through all the moments, through all the years,
Our bond has stayed, unwavering, true,
A friendship that will always renew.

So here's to you, my friend, my heart,
For from the very start, we were never apart.
In every moment, through every season,
You'll forever be my reason.

36. Fourteen

"Isn't 14 too young,
to feel so many emotions?"
I asked myself,
sitting on the floor as the tears welled,
that choking feeling in my throat.

I didnt understand why.
Why do I feel this way?
"You are too young to be sad",
I hear in my head.

I want this feeling to go, to fade,
To leave me in the peace I once made.
A time when joy was simple, pure,
When everything felt safe, secure.

But now it's heavy, too much to bear,
A weight in my chest, a constant stare.
The world moves on, but I stand still,
Caught in the chaos, against my will.

I never took anything; I just want to be,
A kid who smiles, who's finally free.

To laugh without the ache in my heart,
To feel like I'm whole, not falling apart.

I wouldn't dare to tell my family.
Even i do not know where this sadness has rooted from,
but it has taken over,
and has clouded my glasses.

I seemed so uncontrollably happy not too long ago,
in that hazy 2018.
I promise I'm not faking,
it's anything I wish I was.
I wish I can understand, that why do I feel everything, yet
nothing at all.

So I ask for peace, for light in the dark,
To feel again, like I'm a spark.
To have the joy that once was mine,
To find myself in a world that's kind.

"Isn't 14 too young to feel this way?" rings up in my head
again...

37. No-one Understands

"I know it's hard, I understand, Satakshi."
They say it so easily, like it's rehearsed.
Like they've lived my pain,
Like they've carried the weight of my worst days.

But they haven't.
They haven't felt the sting of breaking in silence,
Or the loneliness of screaming in a room full of people
Who only hear their own echoes.

They talk of hope like it's a simple thing,
But they can't feel the storm that it brings.
They don't know the silence I wade through,
The battles inside, the things I undo.

No one understands, and they never can,
The parts of me that break and span.
The quiet wars, the unseen scars,
The spaces between the moon and stars.

They want to fix me, to make me whole,
But they don't know the cracks in my soul.
They never will, for this is mine,

A truth that hides, a life confined.

No one understands, and they never should,
For how could they, when they never would
Walk the roads I've walked alone,
Or hear the whispers I've never known.

They tell me to stay strong, to move on,
As if my heart is something I can switch off.
As if my tears need their permission to fall.

But my pain is mine.
My tears are not for their approval,
Not for them to measure or validate.
They are proof that I've felt deeply,
That I've survived things they will never understand.

So don't tell me how to feel.
Don't tell me my tears aren't justified.
Because if you haven't walked my path,
You don't get to tell me how to heal.

So I stand in the dark, in silence and grace,
Knowing that no one will ever trace
The parts of me I keep unseen,
And perhaps that's where I've always been.

38. Cosmic Eyes

Your eyes, two endless galaxies wide,
Where moonlit dreams and whispers hide.
A nebula of love and light,
Holding dawn and deepest night.

They carry storms, they hold the stars,
Mapping destinies from afar.
In their depths, the cosmos sings,
Of ancient truths and silent angel wings.

A universe within their gaze,
Spinning worlds in golden haze.
Lost in them, I find my way,
Through endless night to break of day.

Each blink, a comet's fiery flight,
A flash of brilliance, burning bright.
With every glance, a distant star,
Guiding me, no matter how far.

The constellations that you weave,
Are stories of the heart you leave.
Galaxies of hope unfold,

A tale of love, both young and old.

The stars collide in soft embrace,
When I look into your sacred face.
In the silence of your cosmic eyes,
I hear the universe's quiet sighs.

They hold the past, the present, too,
Every dream that could come true.
Within those depths, I see the skies,
And in them, I see our future rise.

Through cosmic dust, through astral streams,
We float together in endless dreams.
Your eyes, they are the map, the chart,
Guiding me back to where we start.

The moonlight dances in your gaze,
A thousand suns in endless blaze.
Within those eyes, I see the whole,
The universe, the depths of soul.

So when the night feels far and cold,
I'll look into your eyes of gold,
And find my way, through cosmic streams,
In your gaze, I'll live my dreams.

39. The Need To Run

There are times I want to run,

to chase the wind, to touch the sun.

When every breath feels sharp and deep,

and every sorrow starts to seep.

The weight of days,

the nights that bend but never break.

Yet in the dark, a whisper stays,

soft but strong, it lights my way.

"This is life," the voice explains,

"a path of love, of loss, of pain."

The storms may rage, the skies may weep,

but strength is found where shadows creep.

So I keep walking, step by step,

past broken dreams and words unsaid.

Through shattered dawns and bitter ends,

until the light returns again.

For even pain must bow and fade,

to hearts that choose to rise, unafraid.

40. Distant Friendships

"Do You Miss Me Too?" I asked them one day.
As silence stretched in the shades of grey,
they smiled and said " Our friendship is still the same"
"It's just us who have changed".

But, in their eyes, a truth unsaid.
a quiet ache.
We didn't change - not who we are,
but our friendship faded and left a scar.

How did we get here?
How did the space between us
grow so wide, so unfamiliar?
I hate it.
I hate watching us drift,
like strangers in a place we once called home.

I hate feeling like I lost you,
like our friendship is just a memory now,
a story we stopped telling.
And I wonder,
do you ever miss me at the same time I miss you?
Do you ever reach for your phone,

only to put it down, just like I do?

A bond once whole, now thin as lace,
I wonder, do they even care?
Because,
not all goodbyes are said out loud,
some drift away behind the cloud.

I won't say it.
I won't break the silence.
But I miss you.

So if you ever feel it too,
if you ever want to,
meet me at our old spot.
And maybe we can find our way back.

41. Dumb Conversations

I have no stories left to tell,
no new words to say,
but still, I find myself here,
wanting you to stay.

No grand confessions, no tales to weave,
just silence, soft and pure.
Even if I have nothing to say,
I still want to talk to you.

Even your presence is a beacon in the night,
your words alone case a silver light.
no need to say,
I feel you near in every way.

A quiet love, a sheltering storm,
no spoken vow, no promised plea.
yet still, you stand,
you stay with me.

Through darkest hours, through endless greys,
your presence shines, and lights my way,
no words, no voice, no name,

for love 'unspoken' glows the same.

We could sit in quiet pauses,
let the world just drift away.
No need for words to fill the space,
your presence is enough to stay.

For talking isn't just the words,
it's the comfort in your tone,
it's knowing that I'm not alone,
even when the words are gone.

42. Justified Tears

My Tears Are Mine!
You don't get to tell me my tears don't matter.
That they're wasted, that they mean nothing.
Every drop that falls is proof I've been fighting,
proof that I'm still here, still trying.

You don't know what it took to hold on,
how heavy the pain can be,
how it wraps around my chest,
until breathing feels like a battle.

You don't know the nights I've spent awake,
staring at the ceiling,
wishing the ache in my heart
would finally ease, finally quiet down.

My cries aren't for attention,
they are the sound of a heart refusing to break.
They are the echoes of every word I never said,
every pain I swallowed whole.

My tears are proof, crystal and clear
that I'm toiling to be here,

each drop is a fight,
a silent war I face day and night.

They glisten slowly, yet weigh heavier than a stone,
screaming, shouting about the battles I face alone.

These tears, don't tell I'm weak,
no,
these tears are made of steel,
a testament to tell what I really feel.

Yet, through the rain, I stand,
washing my wounds and my past,
but not to send them away.
For every drop that falls,
is a proof I still chase the dream.

So don't tell me to be quiet.
Don't tell me to move on.
You don't get to decide what hurts me,
what leaves a mark or, what stays.

My tears are mine, and they matter.
Because they are proof that I do too.

43. My Brother

As another year ends,
our memories are fading,
and I'm scared,
to forget you.

Only memories are left with me,
since you left.

I'll miss you forever,
because you were my brother,
and always will be.
And no matter how much time steals from me,
that will never change.

Another year flew by,
and I wish you had been here,
for the big moments,
for the little ones,
for everything in between.

The air is warm,
but not like your presence, of how it was a candle in the dark.
Summers are starting, and I wish you had been here.

But wherever you are,

I hope you know,

I still carry you with me.

44. My Sun

Tell me all of your darknesses and secrets,
the thoughts that creep in the night,
the storms that rage within you,
the weight you try to hide.

Let me hear the scars of stone in your voice,
the swallowed words behind your sighs.
Let me see the tears you never shed,
the fears behind your tired eyes.

And still,
I would look at you like you are the sun.
I never realised how frozen I was,
until you came and made me melt by your beautiful light.
like the light, that warms my skin,
like the golden glow that lingers,
even when the day grows dim.

For even in your deepest night,
you are still the dawn to me.
No darkness could ever change,
the way your light was meant to be for me.

45. I Will

I'm going to make you proud, mumma and papa.
No matter how badly the nights crush me,
No matter how the days turn me sad.

I'll rise beyond my fear inside,
Even when doubt clouds my way.
Even if my voice trembles and shakes,
I'll find my strength to stay.

Like dawn's soft glow, I will unfurl,
breaking free, as my dreams uncurl.

I'll chase the dreams you wished for me,
I'll climb each mountain tall.
Even when my steps feel heavy,
Even if sometimes I fall.

Because your love has shaped my heart,
Your faith has lit my soul.
And though the journey tests my will,
I'll fight to make it whole.

One day, you'll see me standing there,

With all I've worked to be.
And when you smile, so proud and bright,
I'll know,
I have made it, finally.

46. How Can I Ever Forget?

How can I ever forget?
The mundane details drift away,
The clothes I wore, a meal consumed,
Fading like whispers at the close of day.

Yet every moment spent with you,
Is etched in memory, clear and bright,

Your laughter, like a symphony,
The purest melody to ever survey.
Your smile, like a light,
Shining bright from day to night.
Your hair, like an angel,
Kissing your forehead to a deep dwell.

I may lose the echoes of trivial things,
The passing days, the fleeting sound,
But every word, every smile of you
In my heart is forever found.

So even as time erases small details,
Your presence remains forever, and true.

In a world where the ordinary vanishes,

How can I ever forget you?

47. The Silent Giver

I make them laugh, I dry their tears,
I calm their doubts, I ease their fears.
I cheer the loudest when they win,
But who will ask how I have been?

They come to me with broken hearts,
I patch them up, stitch every part.
I stand so strong, they think I'm fine,
But no one sees these cracks in mine.

Do they ever ask me,
What's wrong? or why I had been crying?

I share their dreams, I lift their weight,
I never ask, I never take.
I am the rock, the hand to hold,
Yet here I stand, alone and cold.

At night, I stare into the dark,
An aching void inside my heart.
I give, I love, I try, I stay,
But does someone wish I felt okay?

I muse,
if this is the world, so cold and rude.
Selfish hearts and manners that are blind,
I wonder, do they even see?
or care at all if I wither away quietly?

Maybe one day, they'll understand,
That even those who lend a hand,
Who smile the brightest, shine so true,
Are sometimes wishing,
just to be held.

48. The Ceaseless Show

I've been miserable,
but no one knows.
Guess I've learned to put on a good show.

I smile at the right moments,
laugh when I should,
say, I'm fine—and they believe it.

But the nights feel heavier than they should,
filled with thoughts I can't run away from,
The silence stays,
louder than any words I never say.

Sometimes, I wonder,
if someone looked a little closer,
if they really listened,
would they see through the act?

Would they be able to tell,
how long I have been pretending?

Would they ask again,
if I am fine or not? and actually wait for the real answer?

Or would they just nod,
accept the performance,
and let me play my part again tomorrow?

49. Away, From This World.

Take me away, far from this place,
Where I can live in your warm embrace.
A world where time slows to our tune,
And love glows bright beneath the moon.

A place where whispers fill the air,
And every moment, love we share.
No rush, no fear, no world outside,
Just you and me, side by side.

We'd talk for hours, lost in dreams,
Flowing like rivers, endless streams.
No voices loud, no eyes that pry,
Just you and me beneath the sky.

So take me away, don't let me stay,
In your arms, I'll fade away.
To a life where only love is true,
A world of us, where we can be.

Away, from this world, where no one can see, take me there,
just you and me.

50. Loneliness, Wears My Name

Loneliness knocks, soft at first,
then harder, insistent, like an old friend
who never waits for an invitation.
It slips through the cracks in the door,
settling into my chair, my bed,
filling the spaces left behind.

It wears my sweater,
pulls my blankets tight,
sits beside me at the table,
stirring a cup of nothing.
Its breath fogs the mirror,
its hands rest on my shoulders,
light as a paling memory, heavy as regret.

At night, it croons a tune I almost recognize,
pressing close, whispering stories
of all the people who once stayed,
and all the ones who left.
It knows their names.
It speaks them softly,
like a tune meant to break me.

I tell it to go.
It only smiles.
It has nowhere else to be.
It has made a home of me.

It traces the lines of my palms,
laughs at my emptiness,
fills my pockets with echoes,
my lungs with silence,
my heart with the weight of unspoken things.

It walks with me through crowded streets,
threading its fingers through mine,
invisible but never absent,
turning strangers into reminders,
turning laughter into noise I no longer understand.

Even in sleep, it stays,
folding itself into my dreams,
painting my world in muted grays,
whispering, always whispering.

In my dreams,
it haunts me,
mocks me about the battles I once fought,
tells me tales of people I lost.

I ask god to bring light,
for that I can fade into horizon
from this eclipse of my life.

And when the sun rises,
I wake to find it still there,
waiting, watching,
a shadow that does not fade.

"between The Lines, Forever"

And so, the final page turns, yet the echoes still remain.

BITTERSWEET was never just a book or a story, it was a reflection of love and loss, of fleeting moments and unspoken words, of the quiet ache of change and the beauty in remembering.

To those who have walked through these pages with me, thank you. Your time, your thoughts, and your heart have breathed life into these words. If you found a even a fragment of yourself within these lines, then this journey was worth taking.

May you embrace the bittersweet.

The endings, that carve new beginnings, the goodbyes that whisper of tomorrow, and the love that stays even after the last word is read.

With gratitude and warmth,
Satakshi Pagore.